THE HISTORY OF CUBA
IN 50 EVENTS

Table of Contents

26) 1956 - Castro and Che Begin Invasion of Cuba

27) 1958 - U.S. Withdraws Support for Batista

28) 1959 - Castro Seizes Power

29) 1960 - Cuba Nationalizes American Businesses

30) 1961 - Bay of Pigs Incident

31) 1962 - The Cuban Missile Crisis

32) 1965 - Cuban Communist Party is Formed

33) 1972 - Cuba Joins CMEA

34) 1976 - New Socialist Constitution Adopted

35) 1976 - Cuba Sends Military Aid to Angola

36) 1980 - 250,000 Refugees Flee to the U.S.

37) 1988 - Cuba Withdraws Troops from Angola

38) 1991 - Soviet Advisors Leave Cuba

39) 1993 - U.S. Strengthens Embargo Against Cuba

40) 1994 - U.S./Cuban Refugee Agreement

41) 1996 - Embargo Made Permanent

42) 1998 - Pope John Paul II Visits Cuba

43) 1999 - Elian Gonzalez Legal Battle

44) 2000 - United States Approves Food and Medical Sales in Cuba

45) 2002 - Guantanamo Bay Naval Base Used for Interrogation of Suspected Terrorists

46) 2002 - Former President Jimmy Carter Visits Cuba

47) 2008 - Fidel Castro Resigns

48) 2012 - First Public Religious Holiday since 1959

49) 2014 - Deep-Water Port Project Started by Brazil

50) 2015 - Diplomatic Relations with United States Re stored

Early Cuban History

1) 3100 BCE - First Cuban Settlement

The earliest evidence for human settlement in Cuba dates to approximately 3100 BCE near the modern city of Levisa, which is located in the southeastern region of Cuba. The inhabitants were known to use stone tools and lived the life of hunter-gatherers, meaning that permanent settlement was less favored than easily moveable communities. Over the next several centuries, due to advances in technology and mild weather, these proto-Cuban inhabitants moved from a hunter-gatherer society to an agrarian one. The long growing season allowed the natives (who would later be named the Arawak) to produce a more than ample supply of food for the civilization. In fact, the island of Cuba provided such favorable farming conditions that it played a large part in the economic growth of Spain in the sixteenth century CE.

The Arawak displayed a similar religious structure with many other Central American cultures—ritual sacrifice to appease the gods. This structure makes sense in a pre-industrial culture that was wholly dependent on the weather for the success of their yearly crop, and it is this reality that plays a role in the similarities of early Central American religions.

2) 1492 - Columbus Discovers Cuba

In October 1492 CE, Christopher Columbus and his three-ship expedition reached the island of Hispaniola. After exploring the island, Columbus' crew began venturing to other Caribbean islands. Inevitably, the expedition reached Cuba. Columbus began to trade with the Arawak both in Cuba and Hispaniola, and although they could not provide the riches Columbus sought (he believed he was in China or India), they were able to provision the expedition with fruit, water, and fresh meat.

In 1494, Columbus returned to Cuba as part of his second expedition. Despite Columbus' efforts, the coast of Cuba was not fully mapped until 1509, and for this reason, the Spanish refused to colonize the island until such time as the survey was complete. Prior to the second voyage, Columbus had been given a papal bull (an order from the Pope) to convert the native population of unexplored areas to Catholicism. Columbus brought the beginnings of a wide-spread adoption of Catholicism to the Caribbean, which continues to play a central role in the lives of many people living in Central America.

3) 1511 - First Spanish Settlement

In 1511, Diego de Cuellar, a Spanish explorer, left Hispaniola with orders to conquer Cuba. The first step in accomplishing this was the creation of a permanent settlement on the island, thus allowing a forward staging base for the task. Unsurprisingly, the Arawak were not willing participants in this campaign.

The local chiefs of the Arawak led the people in a guerrilla war against the Spanish. Even after the capture of the chiefs and their executions by fire, it took nearly three years before the Spanish were able to subdue the local population and take control of the island. Eventually, the first Spanish settlement was created at Baracoa. To aid with the settlement efforts, the encomienda system was put in place. This system forcibly relocated the indigenous population of the island into specific zones set aside for their use. This system gave the Spanish the advantage of population control, which was essential for keeping control of the island, and best exploiting the labor of the natives who were now thralls of the Spanish.

4) 1514 - Havana Founded

After the conquest of Cuba, and the establishment of the encomienda system, the Spanish set about colonizing the island. In 1514, the Spanish established Havana, which at the time was a small settlement, but within a few short years would become perhaps the most important port in North America. As the Spanish settled North and Central America, Havana became a stopping point to purchase the provisions necessary for further exploration. Moreover, as the Spanish began to export gold to Spain, Havana became the crossover point where trans-Atlantic ships would bring supplies and return to Spain with gold, while smaller ships would explore North America and send the gold to Havana for export. More important than perhaps any other Spanish settlement, Havana became the economic heart of Cuba and of the Spanish empire in the New World.

As the highest-profile Spanish port in the New World, Havana was often raided by privateers and pirates. The city underwent much turmoil, but the attempts to fortify and rebuild it help explain why the city remained viable for so long, and why today so much of the history of the city can be found in the original buildings that still stand.

5) 1526 - First Slaves Imported

Beyond simply being a staging port for Spanish exploration, Cuba had plentiful food resources. Among the most profitable was cane sugar, which grew in overwhelming abundance on the island. Cane sugar became very popular in Spain and soon other European countries. The demand for sugar grew far beyond what the Arawak population was able to grow, even under the incentive of the Spanish.

Rather than allow an opportunity to pass, the Spanish began importing slaves to Cuba in 1526. The importation of slaves created a Triangle Trade Route, where slaves were imported to Cuba, the slaves grew and harvested sugar (and other crops), then the goods were shipped to Europe for final assembly or processing, before finished goods were shipped to Africa to help pay for slaves to be transported to the New World.

This system was so expeditious and efficient that many slaves who would be sent to the United States had actually been slaves in Cuba first. Thus, the history of slavery in America, and the slave trade in Britain and Belgium, was intimately tied to the slave trade in Cuba. And, much like in Cuba, slaves transported to America would be purchased to farm a cash crop that was far more labor-intensive than locals could farm alone.

6) 1762 - Britain Captures Havana

From 1756 to 1763, the British Empire was engaged in a conflict known variously as the Seven Years' War, the Third Carnatic War, the French and Indian War, or the Pomeranian War. This conflict was largely between Britain and France. The British were seeking total control over North America, particularly America and Canada, as well as limiting the power of the French throughout the world. At the same time, France sought reparations for the 30 Years' War that had taken place in the previous century.

As a part of this conflict, battles took place in America, the Caribbean, Southeast Asia, and Africa. The British were very successful in their endeavor, as their navy was the premier fleet in the world, and this allowed the British to successfully fight on multiple fronts. During the battle in the Caribbean, the British captured Havana. Thanks to its strategic value, the city was claimed by the British, even though the Spanish were not the primary targets of British aggression. In the same vein, England also captured the Spanish-held Philippine Islands.

The capture of Cuba demonstrates precisely how important Cuba had become in the growth of North America. Although the British were not primarily interested in Cuba for its agricultural bounty, it did provide a bargaining chip in the negotiations that the British knew would inevitably follow the combat phase of the conflict. Further, the capture of Havana gave the Spanish pause, as this capture made the cost of war with

England untenable for the Spanish. As such, the British faced significantly less opposition from the Spanish than might have otherwise occurred. Simply by virtue of location, Havana became an important piece in the much larger war that took place all over the world during that short period of time.

7) 1763 - Treaty of Paris Signed

On February 10, 1763, the Seven Years' War came to an end. The British, after successfully defeating both the Spanish and the French, joined its enemy states in Paris to formalize the end of the war. Under the terms of the Treaty of Paris, France surrendered most of its territorial holdings in North America, particularly Canada and the Ohio River Valley. In exchange for Florida, the British returned Havana and Manila (the capital of Philippines) to Spain.

After the Treaty of Paris was signed, many Cubans began to long for independence and, as Cuba was responsible for paying a large portion of the Spanish war debt, began to question the right of Spanish rule on the island. This longing would begin a process that lasted almost 150 years and would culminate in the independence of Cuba, although the country itself would not play a role in its own independence. Instead, that role would belong to the United States, which would set Cuba free after claiming possession at the end of the Spanish-American War. Ultimately, thanks to its strategic location, Cuba had become involved in a conflict not of its own making—a trend which would continue into the twentieth century.

8) 1765 - Sugar Boom Begins

At the conclusion of the Seven Years' War, the Spanish began to fortify the city of Havana to ensure that if a future conflict broke out, the city would be safe from invasion. The Spanish fortifications were of such a massive nature that Havana became the most heavily defended city in the New World. This level of protection also ensured a time of great peace in Cuba. This peace led to a drastic upswing in the production of agricultural goods, notably sugar.

Thanks to the Treaty of Paris, relations between Spain and England were improving. As a part of this relationship, the Spanish revoked their monopoly on the sugar trade, allowing the British to purchase sugar directly from Cuba. As the British had turned tea into part of their culture, the demand for sugar skyrocketed. The British were pleased to buy sugar directly, as the cost was reduced. The Cubans in turn were thrilled to have more trading partners, and the Spanish were pleased to gain extra revenue through the taxes raised.

Despite being thousands of miles from either Spain or Britain, Cuba continued to play a major role in world events that gave the country far greater influence than its size or location would indicate.

9) 1810 - First Constitution Drafted

As the world moved on from the conflict during the Seven Years' War, many Cubans sought their independence. From time to time, small groups would arise in an attempt to gain control over the island. And in 1810, Joaquin Infante, a leader in a small resistance movement, wrote the first constitution for Cuba. The constitution declared Cuba to be independent, established an aristocracy, laid out a class system for citizens based on skin color, and promoted Catholicism as the official religion. This constitution, although perhaps not espousing the values cherished by modern societies, was in fact a real constitution that provided a framework for independent governance of Cuba.

But, like many attempts before it, Infante's rebellious cause was defeated; he and other leaders were sent to Spain to be imprisoned. Despite this, Infante's actions became a rallying point for other liberationists. His attempt at self-rule provided the impetus for continued rebellion that would remain until Cuba's liberation in 1902.

10) 1868 - Ten Years War Begins

From 1868 until 1878, Cuba was engaged in a war with Spain over control of the island. The Cuban leader was Carlos Cespedes, who organized wealthy farmers and other important Cuban businessmen. Cespedes even tried to get Cuban slaves to join the revolt, although many of them were skeptical of his promises.

Within the first three days of conflict, Cespedes' forces captured the city of Bayamo. Although the city was retaken after months of fighting, it was destroyed as a result.

During the course of the war, the Spanish were forced to impose ever stricter laws on the Cubans still under their control. As an example, any male over the age of 15 who was found outside of the plantation they lived on without valid reason would be executed as a suspected rebel. If women were found outside of the plantation, they would be forcibly relocated to camps within Spanish-controlled cities. As much as the Spanish were not prepared to fight a guerrilla war, the Cubans were not prepared to face the suffering of their families under the heel of their colonial overlords.

After ten long, bloody years, the war was finally brought to an end with the Pact of Zanjon, which attempted to provide better social and economic conditions for Cubans. Tensions continued to run high between both sides, and eventually the Little War was fought in 1879. These tensions would come to a final head during the Spanish-American War beginning in 1895.

11) 1886 - Slavery Abolished

Following in the footsteps of Britain and America, Spain brought about an end to its practice of slavery in 1886. Although Spain had no slaves in Europe, it is estimated that the country brought over a million slaves to Cuba and the West Indies during the period of 1500-1886. The vast bulk of these slaves either worked in sugar cane fields or were shipped to the United States to grow tobacco and cotton.

The abolition of slavery had an unintended consequence, which was that the freedom of the slaves inspired Cuban citizens to reexamine their relationship with Spain, leading them to reach the conclusion that independence was not beyond their reach.

Over the next decade, discontent on the part of Cubans continued to rise. Conversely, when the Spanish liberated their slaves, it was hoped that freedom would ally the former slaves to the Spanish, and not to Cubans. To some extent this proved effective, as the population of slaves was large enough to be a decisive factor for whichever side the former slaves chose to ally with in a future conflict. In the end, however, the tension between Spain and Cuba grew until the issue of slave assistance was no longer the leading factor in the conflict. When this occurred, Cuba and Spain would once again go to war.

12) 1895 - Spanish-American War Begins

When the tension between Spain and Cuba finally degenerated into war in 1895, it seemed unlikely that Cuba had any hope of winning freedom. But the United States, operating under the Monroe Doctrine, decided to take up the part of the Cubans. This doctrine declared that the United States had preeminence in New World affairs, and that it, not Spain, would determine the outcome for Cuba. As such, the United States declared war on Spain.

During the course of the war, the U.S. invaded Cuba. It was then that Theodore Roosevelt and his so-called Rough Riders made a name for themselves during the Battle of San Juan Hill. The United States also captured the Philippines from Spain. At war's end, the U.S. claimed Cuba, the Philippines (for which it paid 20 million dollars), and other New World holdings. The United States set up a military governor to run operations in Cuba until such time as direct governance could be restored.

The end goal was an independent Cuba that would be a participant in the North American community of nations. Cuba's long struggle for independence was almost at an end; with the help of the United States, the dream would become a reality.

13) 1898 - The United States Gains Control of Cuba

After gaining control of Cuba at the end of the Spanish-American War, the United States sought a plan by which Cuba could be given enough stability to create a government capable of self-rule.

In 1898, the Teller Amendment was passed. This amendment prohibited America from claiming Cuba as a territorial possession. A military governor was installed in Cuba to ensure that the transition from a Spanish to Cuban government was smooth and efficient. The United States agreed to remove all of its forces from Cuba when Cuba agreed that the U.S. would be allowed to intervene in Cuban affairs for the protection of the Caribbean country as a whole. Further, the Platt Amendment, as it was called, gave the United States the right to lease land from Cuba for military bases. The largest portion of land that was leased to the U.S. was the land located on Guantanamo Bay, where the United States Navy maintains facilities to the present day.

Over the next two decades, the U.S. would intervene in Cuban affairs, citing the Teller Amendment as justification. Despite the intentions of the United States, many Cubans resented the presence of America in Cuba. This presence was seen as a pretext for outright domination of the island. As such, Cuban-American relations were tinged with tension, although not of the severity during the end of Spanish rule. Eventually, with the advent of World War I, most of America's involvement with Cuba came to a halt, giving the country the independence it had so long desired.

Modern Cuban History

14) 1902 - Cuba Gains Independence

In 1900, the United States oversaw an election for Cuba's legislative assembly. This assembly drafted Cuba's constitution from late 1900 until early 1901, at which point the assembly voted to adopt the constitution. At that time, the United States required Cuba to endorse the Platt Amendment, which would prevent Cuba from making treaties with foreign powers if that treaty would limit Cuba's freedom or self-rule. Cuba would also provide land to be leased to the U.S. for military bases. When Cuba assented, the United States began withdrawing its troops in preparation for Cuba to take over its own defense.

On December 31, 1901, Cuba held its first presidential election; the only candidate was Tomas Palma, who was an American citizen at the time. After the election, Palma moved to Cuba, and the United States withdrew its forces. Palma was an able ruler, and set Cuba on a path toward economic growth and military security. But the Cuban people were so terrified of the possibility that Palma might seek to become a dictator or king that they staged a revolt when Palma attempted to extend his time in office after his first elected term. This revolt would lead to another American incursion into Cuban life in 1906.

15) 1906 - United States Re-occupies Cuba

When riots began at the end of President Palma's first term in office, the United States decided to step in and restore order. The re-occupation began in 1906, under President Theodore Roosevelt's guidance. William Howard Taft, who would become America's president in 1909, went to Cuba to work out a peaceful resolution to the situation. Palma agreed to retire from service, and the United States installed a governor for Cuba, Charles Magoon, who would continue to serve as governor throughout the three-year occupation.

During this time, Agustin Veloz and Francisco Rosales formed the Cuban Communist Party. Although the party would remain small and powerless for almost 40 years, it would eventually become the ruling party in Cuba. While not always the case, many countries including Cuba had no communist party to speak of until external events made life so untenable that communism seemed a valid means of self-rule and independence.

This occupation by the United States established a pattern that would not be broken until after the Cuban Missile Crisis. The pattern was simply that America would intervene in internal Cuban affairs, which would cause Cuban citizens to become upset, lead to more unrest, which in turn would lead to further intervention and so on, in a continuing spiral. For many Cubans the idea of communism seemed to present the only path to separation from the United States.

16) 1908 - Cuban Elections Held

After two years of occupation, Cuba held presidential elections once again in 1908. Jose Gomez was elected president, and with his election, the United States decided to proceed with the withdrawal of their troops. Gomez was president until 1912 when Mario Menocal assumed the position.

In 1912, the government had to deal with another uprising; to protect the supply of sugar, the United States entered Cuba as a mediator. The American troops left the country once the uprising was past and allowed Menocal to continue governing. Under his supervision, Cuban sugar production increased markedly, and profits from sugar likewise rose. When Menocal was elected for a second term there was another uprising, this time led by a group called the Partido Independiente de Color, or PIC. Once again, the United States sent troops into Cuba. Symptomatically and problematically, Cuba was once again disallowed to manage its internal affairs.

A pattern has emerged in Cuban history where, although it occupies a strategic location, it has relative weakness compared to major nations, making it easy prey for outside control. Although the United States allowed elections to go on, they would continue sending troops into Cuba at the least provocation, which indicates that America saw Cuba as a satellite at that point in history.

17) 1912 - U.S. Gives Aid in Putting Down Protests

Menocal's second election proved to be troublesome for Cuba. In 1912, The PIC began stirring up rebellion in Cuba. Made up entirely of former Cuban slaves who were of African descent, the PIC identified as a highly liberal political party, stressing social and economic equality. This party felt ignored by the aims of other Cuban patriots like Jose Marti who sought Cuban independence, but even Marti seemed to advocate a position that all Cubans should concern themselves with being Cuban, and not on promoting their ethnic equality.

Marti and others ignored the PIC, and in 1912 the country was faced with the looming election of Menocal, whom many believed was unconcerned about their welfare. As such, the PIC began agitating against the election of Menocal, and eventually sought to establish its own supremacy. This rebellion was quickly and harshly put down. The leaders of the PIC were arrested and sent to Spain to be imprisoned.

As agreed in the Platt Amendment, the United States had the right to send troops into Cuba to protect the peace, as well as American interests in the region. With the help of the U.S. military, the PIC was quickly outmanned and arrested. Once again, America's incursion into Cuba had the effect of uniting many nationalists against American aid.

18) 1917 - Cuba Enters World War I

The twentieth century had its share of catastrophic events, but of all of those, none had such an impact as the two world wars. The day after America joined World War I, Cuba declared war on Germany. Due to marked lack of ground troops or transports, Cuba did not send troops to Europe. But the militarization of Cuba prevented German submarines from patrolling the Caribbean. This guard duty was essential to the American war effort as it allowed the port of New Orleans to operate more or less unchallenged.

As we have already seen, Cuba once again played a much larger role than its station would indicate and, due to its ties with America, was able to produce a meaningful effort on behalf of the Allies in World War I. It has even been proposed that without Cuba, Mexico would have heeded the Zimmermann telegram, and perhaps attempted to invade the United States. Due to the mobilization of a U.S.-friendly Cuba, however, it is thought that Mexico was unwilling to leave itself undefended against Cuba while attacking the United States. If true, this means that Cuba played a direct role in America's entrance into World War I, and thus, the defeat of Germany.

19) 1925 - Machado Dictatorship

In 1925, Gerardo Machado was elected president of Cuba. He wanted to modernize the country, and he put in place a plan to improve infrastructure so that Cuba could catch up with its neighbors. When his term ended, he was unable to be reelected as stated in Cuba's constitution. So, instead of returning power to the people, Machado held on to his position, naming himself dictator.

Strangely, given its historical reaction to coups is Cuba, the United States did not interfere with Machado as he sought to consolidate his power. Machado built the Capitol building and improved the University of Havana. But after protests occurred there, Machado had the university closed so that no more challenges to his authority could come from students.

In order to ensure his continued reign, Machado forced several changes to the Cuban constitution so that he might lawfully maintain power. As time went on, Machado's abuses of power grew to the point that he was overthrown by Fulgencio Batista, a soldier who persuaded the army to follow him and depose Machado. The end of Machado's reign set off a long chain of dictatorial leaders in Cuba, and each grew to abuse power more than the preceding dictator. This pattern continued until the elevation of Fidel Castro to president in 1959.

20) 1925 - Creation of the Cuban Socialist Party

In opposition to Machado, as well as previous presidents, a faction of Cubans began to express their desire for a more egalitarian society. As with most societies in which a socialist party emerges, Cuba was undergoing a broadening gap between the wealthy and the impoverished in 1925. Further, the gap between those with power and those without was also widening. Unsurprisingly then, a small group of Cubans formed the Socialist Party.

This party was not socialist in the Robert Owen sense, but more in the Marx/Engels sense, meaning that the Socialist Party espoused views much closer to communism than socialism. However, the word communism had the connotation of anarchy and, as such, gained little respect in most western countries. Meanwhile, socialism sounded almost progressive, meaning that it had a greater base of support than otherwise would have been the case.

In time, communist leaders such as Castro would lead this party to ultimate power in Cuba. As was the case in most countries that eventually turned toward a communist system of government, had the government in Cuba been run with marginally more concern for the will of the people, the communist party would never have gained power and would have merely been another side note to history. Instead, the modern of history of Cuba is so tied up with communism that one cannot separate the two.

21) 1934 - Batista Overthrows Machado

Machado had become so unpopular by 1934 that several liberal rebel groups banded together and formed a provisional government. This government claimed legitimacy, although the Machado government remained. And so, two governments, both claiming power, strove against each other for much of 1934. At the same time, Cuban Sergeant Fulgencia Batista formed a conservative anti-government coalition.

With support of the United States, who found Batista to be the best alternative to Machado, Batista was able to overthrow both the provisional government and the Machado government. From 1934 to 1940, Batista worked to reinstate a stable government capable of governing Cuba. Batista worked to provide free elections; during his tenure in the 1930s, a constitution was adopted. From all outward appearances, Batista was the perfect candidate to oversee the Cuban government. This short, stable period allowed Cubans to continue developing infrastructure and agriculture—two areas of commerce that had been neglected during the chaos under Machado.

During this time, the United States largely left Cuba to its own devices as the threat of war in Europe loomed ever larger. Throughout the New World, the late 1930s was a time to rebuild after the crisis of the Great Depression which had taken its toll on much of North and Central America. Under Batista, Cuba was able to start a program to recovery, and it seemed that all was well.

22) 1940 - Constitution Adopted

The constitution adopted by Cuba in 1940 was a very modern, democratic document. The constitution guaranteed that a democratic republic would continue to exist in Cuba. The constitution also ensured that the judicial branch would remain independent, thus separating the branches of government. It established the levels of representation in the congress and senate, and a court specifically empowered to oversee labor disputes. Further, the constitution granted a great deal of authority to local governments, particularly in regards to taxes and oversight. Historically, the governor of a province had great authority over local matters, but the new constitution eliminated this in order to shift as much power as possible to lower levels of government.

Learning the lessons of the revolts of previous years, the new constitution attempted to give power back to the people so that they would in turn submit to the national government on a more permanent basis, thus enabling a stable, prosperous nation. Given the abuses of power that would begin in the next decade, the constitution was remarkable in that it appeased the vast majority of Cubans for most of the 1940s.

23) 1944 - Batista Retires

After serving his country for a decade, Fulgencia Batista retired from public service at the end of his presidential term. Despite Batista's popularity, the Cuban people chose to elect Ramon San Martin, rather than Carlos Zayas, who had been Batista's choice. As the president at the end of World War II, San Martin oversaw an economic boom, as money that countries had been diverting to their war efforts was suddenly available again.

When soldiers returned home, many sought the little luxuries, such as sugar, meaning that the demand for Cuban sugar cane rose drastically. This led to a period of great economic prosperity, and San Martin embarked on a program of infrastructure upgrades, enabling Cuba to become one of the most modern nations in the world. Thanks to the work of the San Martin government, the Cuban people were able to experience economic prosperity far beyond what anyone had imagined possible. As the standard of living rose, people began to expect the luxuries that they enjoyed, and, when the sugar boom ended, as all economic booms do, the people were so displeased with a return to an older way of life that they began to blame the San Martin government. As time passed, this discontent grew, which would eventually lead to another revolution.

24) 1952 - Batista Seizes Power Again

Prior to the presidential election of 1952, the government had returned to much of the corruption that had plagued Cuba throughout the 1920s and 1930s. Unsurprisingly, the people began to search for alternatives. One of the leading candidates was the Orthodox Party, which ran a campaign of anti-corruption. Unfortunately, the Orthodox Party candidate committed suicide, leaving a relative vacuum in the election cycle.

Fulgencia Batista, former president of Cuba, had decided to run once more in an attempt to curb the excesses in government, but he was not expected to garner many votes. However, with the death of the Orthodox candidate, no one emerged who could challenge him. Instead of proceeding with the election cycle, Batista simply took control of the government. Many Cubans were accepting of these actions, as Batista had been seen as an honorable president.

In 1953, Batista allowed a presidential election to occur, and his victory in this election made him the legitimate president of Cuba. Under Batista, working wages rose, much to the joy of the general populace. Still, the Batista government was plagued with corruption. A young politician named Fidel Castro would seize on this corruption, attempting a coup in 1953. Castro's emergence as a major political player marked the beginning of the end of democracy in Cuba for almost 50 years.

25) 1953 - Castro Attempts a Coup

When Batista seized power in 1952, a young politician named Fidel Castro petitioned the court to depose Batista. However, the court would not hear the case, and Castro, fearing increasing corruption, took matters into his own hands. With his brother Raul and some of their supporters, Castro attempted to capture a military barracks. Castro was caught and sentenced to 15 years in prison. But in 1955 many political prisoners were released by the Batista government, including Castro. Batista was aware of the growing discontent among his citizens and believed that releasing political prisoners would calm the masses.

Castro chose to relocate to Mexico, in order to better plan his next move. During his time in Mexico, Castro met Che Guevara. Che, who was already renowned as a revolutionary in his own right, helped fuel the passion of Castro and saw an opportunity to gain a position of power for himself. Che saw himself as a perpetuator of revolution and sought to fight the forces of democracy, which he believed to be ultimately corrupt. Che and Castro plotted together in order to assure the greatest likelihood of success, and, as history demonstrates, their planning ultimately paid off.

26) 1956 - Castro and Che Begin Invasion of Cuba

Castro and Che returned to Cuba in 1956. When they landed, most of the revolutionaries were captured by the Batista government. Castro and Che escaped and fled into the mountains. True to Che's roots, the forces of Castro began to engage in guerrilla combat with the Batistan forces. In rural areas, Castro's forces were given aid, as many poor farmers saw Castro as a means to increase their social standing. As is almost always the case, Castro's forces grew slowly because wealthier groups did not agree with Castro's methods.

Simultaneously the Batista government began cracking down on any suspicious activity to such an extent that the United States began to impose trade sanctions on Batista. A diplomat was sent to persuade Batista to leave Cuba of his own volition, but Batista declined. From then until 1959, Batista was largely on his own, fighting against the forces of Castro while also fighting against the growing discontent of his people. Several other groups rose up against Batista, notably the socialist/communist party. The communists, while seeking to overthrow Batista, refused to join with Castro as they did not share his beliefs or vision for ruling Cuba. Ultimately, Fidel Castro would be successful, and those who opposed him would pay for their actions during the revolution.

27) 1958 - U.S. Withdraws Support for Batista

As the Cuban Revolution dragged on, Batista's government, determined to maintain power, began committing a series of human and civil rights violations against his people. This was done to prevent aid being given to either Castro or the communists. Batista's actions, however, caused the United States to send emissaries to Batista that pleaded with him to leave Cuba. Determined to outlast Castro and restore his peace to Cuba, Batista refused. His treatment of Cuban citizens grew worse despite of the request of the United States.

Fearing the need to invade Cuba yet again, the United States attempted a new tactic. The U.S. began a systematic embargo of Cuban goods, and, as the United States was Cuba's most important trading partner, this embargo caused great damage to Cuba. The hope was that the people, in fear of starvation, would rise against Batista. Instead, the people blamed the U.S., a move which Castro seized upon. As he decried the United States and Batista, more and more people began to rally behind his cause. Batista lost what little support he had; facing a military coup, he fled Cuba in 1959, paving the way for Castro to seize power.

28) 1959 - Castro Seizes Power

When Batista fled Cuba, Castro immediately seized power. Not favored by the United States or many of his own people, Castro began his reign in a very untenable position. In order to solidify his power, Castro began a series of reprisals against his enemies, as well as those who had also sought power during the Revolution. Castro installed Che as the head of a tribunal to oversee justice for those who had committed crimes during the Revolution. Unsurprisingly, most of Castro's opponents were found guilty of one crime or another and were either given extensive prison sentences or were executed outright. The United States, which had supported Batista throughout much of his time in power, was instantly displeased with Castro's actions. Castro was very much opposed to American influence in Cuba and sought to begin a war against America in order to remove all traces of American power from Cuba.

By 1962, America had imposed yet another trade embargo on Cuba, banning the sale of any Cuban goods in the United States. Castro used these actions to further strengthen his grip on power. Thus began a pattern that would remain in place until 2015, when diplomatic relations were restored. Under this pattern, the U.S. would speak harshly about Castro and tighten the embargo without being willing to commit troops, and Castro would decry American capitalism, without committing actions that would spur the United States to military action—as Castro knew he could not withstand.

Beginning with this embargo on Cuban goods, Castro began searching for an ally in his fight against America. He found that ally in the Soviet Union.

29) 1960 - Cuba Nationalizes American Businesses

In an attempt to improve the Cuban economy without diverting resources to infrastructure programs, Castro sought a quick and easy means of economic recovery. Castro, being particularly angry at the United States, decided to seize ownership of any American businesses in Cuba and nationalize them. In other words, Castro placed American businesses under the management of the Cuban government, without paying the companies for their losses.

Although this seizure led to a short-term economic increase, the resulting American embargo meant that even though Castro could produce a great deal of goods, Cuba had no trading partner that could afford to buy those goods. As a result, Castro's short-term solution turned out to be a long-term nightmare. However, as Castro could not afford to appear weak, he was unwilling to return the businesses or to compensate the owners for their losses. As the embargo deepened and Castro remained unwilling to cooperate, the United States began planning an operation to overthrow Castro.

One difficulty in this plan was that by 1961 Cuba had become friendly with the Soviet Union, even though Castro privately detested communism. Castro was pragmatic enough to realize that the Soviet Union was perhaps his only option for remaining free of the United States, and as such he was willing to behave as if he was a communist supporter, despite his previous political stance. Castro's alliance with the USSR made America's plans for revolution difficult and necessitated a shift in strategy.

30) 1961 - Bay of Pigs Incident

By 1961, it was clear to the United States that Castro needed to be removed from power. Not only was Castro repressing his people, but he was making increasingly friendly overtures towards the Soviet Union. As 1961 was the height of the arms race during the Cold War, the United States was unwilling to do anything that might anger the Soviets into a direct conflict. Instead, the U.S. turned to its own Central Intelligence Agency for a plan.

The CIA realized that, by training a group of insurgents who would invade Cuba and start a rebellion, the United States could deny any involvement, thus appeasing the Soviets. The CIA began training a group of Cuban refugees in Guatemala. The plan was that this group would land in Cuba and lead angry Cuban patriots against Castro and the Cuban army. The CIA supplied these soldiers with weapons and training.

On April 16, 1961, the invasion was launched. The invaders quickly overwhelmed the local militia, which necessitated calling on the army to assist. Castro personally led the military to defeat the invaders. Once captured, the invaders were publicly interrogated, and it wasn't long until the CIA's involvement in the matter became exposed. When this happened, Castro quickly and vocally declared support of the Soviet Union. This declaration of support led to the Cuban Missile Crisis in 1962.

31) 1962 - The Cuban Missile Crisis

In the 1960s, the United States and the Soviet Union were engaged in an arms race. Both sides had developed weapons capable of destroying entire cities and were beginning to deploy them. The U.S. positioned missiles close enough to Russia that Moscow had become a target. In response, the Soviets sought to balance the situation.

Cuba, having very recently befriended the Soviets, was pressured into allowing Russian missiles to be based in Cuba. The United States found out about this, issued Russia an ultimatum, and prepared to blockade Cuba. This blockade was to prevent Soviet nuclear warheads from reaching Cuba and being mated to missiles. The U.S. threatened to sink any Soviet ship that passed the line. The ship, carrying warheads, turned around just before crossing the blockade line. The U.S. agreed to remove the missiles that could target Moscow, and the Soviet Union pledged to remove their missiles from Cuba.

In the aftermath of the crisis, where both sides came unbelievably close to a nuclear exchange, the USSR began sending supplies and aid to Cuba. The United States, reacting to Cuba's part in the crisis, strengthened the embargo against Cuba. Once again, Cuba found itself in the midst of international events far greater than its small size would indicate.

32) 1965 - Cuban Communist Party is Formed

In the wake of Castro's ascension to power, anyone who opposed him was quickly suppressed. Among those who faced reprisal from Castro were political parties that had not aided him in his war and other organizations that had not shared the views of their leader.

As a result of these purges, Cuba had a single political party left by 1965. This party was largely composed of its original members and those who had established their credentials in the aftermath of the revolution. The party's identity had become a mirror of the mind of Castro. As such, it was fluid, and subject to change. In the wake of the strengthened alliance between Cuba and Russia, the party was renamed the Communist Party to demonstrate solidarity with the Soviet Union. This was a pragmatic decision on the part of Castro. Although Castro did not espouse communist views (at least not like those in the Soviet Union), he understood that this change would impress the Russians and lead to an increase in trade and defense, things Castro had been seeking.

33) 1972 - Cuba Joins CMEA

The Council for Mutual Economic Aid was a Soviet-sponsored economic cooperative organization. Its purpose was to provide a trading bloc that would support other communist countries. As the United States' embargo on Cuba lengthened, the country was desperate for enough trade to allow it to remain self-sustaining.

In 1972, Cuba joined CMEA in order to boost its trade and receive support from other communist countries. In response, the United States once again tightened the trade embargo on Cuba, hoping that this would convince Cuba to turn from its communist allies and instead ally itself with the West. In typical fashion, Castro used the continued blockade to present himself as the only defense against the encroaching capitalists. In response, the CMEA gave increased aid to Cuba, allowing it to continue surviving the American embargo.

But the CMEA was not able to provide enough support for Cuba to maintain all aspects of its society; Cuban infrastructure continued to age and deteriorate. As always, people began to complain about the conditions, and those who complained too loudly were arrested and sent to prison.

34) 1976 - New Socialist Constitution Adopted

After almost 15 years of ruling by fiat, Castro's government sought to legitimize itself fully in the eyes of the world. The government drafted a new, socialist constitution. A referendum was needed to pass the constitution, and almost 98 percent of the voters approved it. Included in the constitution was the right for the government to control the marketplace (by its very definition the essence of socialism). It called for universal education and healthcare. The constitution also called for all media to be under the supervision of the government, and for the government to have oversight with respect to organized religion.

Although the constitution did not change the behavior of the Castro government, it did permit Castro to stop ruling by decree, which gave Cuba somewhat a better reputation among peer states. This constitution was later amended to provide that the socialist system in Cuba was to exist in perpetuity and could not be revoked. These changes would insure that Castro could never be forced to abdicate his power, and that only through death or retirement would his power pass to his successor.

35) 1976 - Cuba Sends Military Aid to Angola

In 1975, Angola was given independence by Portugal. Immediately, fighting broke out over the right to create and maintain a government. Major countries around the world sent aid and support to the various sides of the conflict—in this way, Angola became a part of the indirect conflict that was a key feature of the Cold War.

In order to demonstrate its strength and commitment to communism, Cuba sent troops to Angola in 1976, just as other countries had begun bringing their troops home. Tired of war after Vietnam, neither the Soviet Union nor the United States were willing to commit any major resources. Into that vacuum came Cuba. Determined to make an international name for itself, the country intervened in the conflict. But in helping to take control of much of southern Angola, Cuba was soon resented by the Angolans. Before long, Cuba found itself mired in a conflict that was in many ways similar to Vietnam, albeit on a smaller scale.

The actions taken by Cuba during the war did not gain it any favor, as most countries felt that Cuba had interfered in a matter that it did not have the strength to adjudicate. In the long run, Cuba spent money and resources that it did not have in order to make an impression that failed to impress. As the Soviets and Americans learned in Vietnam, aiding a conflict merely for prestige never ends satisfactorily or with victory.

36) 1980 - 250,000 Refugees Flee to the U.S.

During the early 1980s Cuba underwent a time of crisis known as the "Special Period." By the 1980s, the Soviet Union was struggling to match the United States in military might, and this led the Soviets to increase the size of their military. The money spent on defense was taken, in part, from the trade budget of the Soviet Union. Cuba, having the USSR as its primary trading partner, was left largely without a national income. As much as 80% of Cuba's trade was gone, and it crippled the Cuban economy.

Already tired of living under privation due to the Castro government, many Cubans sought an alternative to life in their homeland. From 1980 to 1990, estimates indicate that somewhere between 250,000 and 1,000,000 Cubans fled to the United States. A large proportion of these immigrants settled in Florida, where many Cubans had settled previously, and established a community. With the influx of this wave of immigrants, Cubans began to make up a significant percent of the population in Florida, and, when these immigrants received citizenship, made up a large voting bloc, particularly in urban areas like Miami.

These Cuban-Americans then paved the way for move immigrants, prompting attempts at immigration reform, particularly in Florida. Castro, of course, wanted these people back; however, the United States did not want to send these people back to likely imprisonment. And so the problem of Cuban immigration was never settled, and both Cuba and the United States continue to deal with the effects of immigration.

37) 1988 - Cuba Withdraws Troops from Angola

Despite the economic hardships of the early 1980s, Cuba remained committed to helping communist forces in Angola. But as the full effects of the Special Period were felt, Castro began to hesitate in regards to his commitment to Angola. With much civil unrest at home, coupled with a ruined economy, Castro needed to divert resources to aid his people if he desired to remain in power. And after twelve years of support for the communist forces in Angola, Castro brought his troops home in 1988.

Although the withdrawal lasted for three years, the large-scale support that Angola had enjoyed came to an end. The futility of the conflict was such that it continued until 2002. Castro had hoped to appease his people by returning the troops to Cuba, but the reality ended up being far different. Castro, instead of undertaking an infrastructure improvement project, which might have allowed Cuba to rebuild its economy, spent the money in wasteful ways. The discontent of his people grew. Yet another wave of immigrants left for the United States, and Castro began a series of crackdowns against his people in an attempt to exert control over them and prevent further refugees from leaving. This pattern of repression and immigration would continue until Castro retired in 2008.

38) 1991 - Soviet Advisors Leave Cuba

In 1991, due to economic, political, and social forces, the Soviet Union disbanded, and communism was brought to an end in Russia. During the Special Period, the USSR had left military advisors in Cuba to help the country prepare defenses and plot methods to support the communist cause. With the dissolution of the Soviet Union, however, Russia lost the will to keep advisors in Cuba.

When the withdrawal occurred, civil unrest followed, as many Cubans saw an opportunity for change. Sadly, Castro had other plans, and continued his oppression of the people. While Cuba had been an important part of world events during the Cold War, the withdrawal of the Soviet Union left it a hollow shell. With no real trading or military partners, Cuba became a backwater nation that lagged far behind peer nations in the region and around the world. Castro tried to paint a picture for the people that blamed the United States and Russia, but Cubans realized that responsibility for the state of the nation lay at the feet of Castro's poor decision making throughout the previous decades. Unsurprisingly, another wave of immigration to the United States occurred.

39) 1993 - U.S. Strengthens Embargo Against Cuba

In the wake of Castro's continued oppression against his people, the United States once again stiffened the embargo against Cuba. The U.S. hoped that by making conditions in Cuba even worse, the people would become angry enough to overthrow Castro—at which point the United States could offer aid. But, in a demonstration of his talent for self-preservation, Castro diverted resources to his most trusted supporters, many of whom held military roles.

By keeping the military happy, Castro ensured that he would be protected in the event of a coup or assassination attempt. Many Cubans in the United States began to call for aid to Cuba as opposed to the embargo, but the U.S. kept with its historical policy by refusing while Castro remained in power. Castro, in the wake of these new regulations, tightened his grip on the people of Cuba, no longer pretending to be concerned with the well-being of his citizens but rather simply concerned with staying in power.

The question must be asked at this point: why did the United States not eliminate Castro? Simply put, at that time the U.S. maintained a policy of not assassinating the leaders of recognized countries, even if that leader is doing harm to his people. As a result, the United States had to find other means of removing Castro from power, as it was unwilling to remove Castro by force.

40) 1994 - U.S./Cuban Refugee Agreement

In an attempt to improve relations with Cuba and to stop the flood of Cuban immigrants into the United States, the U.S. reached an immigration reform agreement with Cuba in 1994. Known as the "wet foot/dry foot" agreement, it stipulated that any Cuban found in international waters (wet foot) would be returned to Cuba, and that any immigrant who reached the United States (dry foot) would be allowed to remain and given a quick path to citizenship. This agreement was designed to incentivize Castro to help patrol his home waters, and in that way aid the effort to stop more refugees from fleeing.

This agreement led to further talks in 1995 and 1996, but these talks broke down when Castro refused several key demands of the United States. Castro's answer to the refugee crisis was fairly predictable—he simply issued severe punishments for returned refugees. Castro's refusal to cooperate fully with the United States led to the embargo once again being stiffened by the U.S. Bill Clinton, the president of the United States at the time, sought desperately to repair relations with Cuba as he understood the value of international cooperation; Castro, given his history with the United States, refused.

41) 1996 - Embargo Made Permanent

Following the breakdown of immigration talks with Cuba and Castro's resulting oppression, the United States decided to make the Cuban embargo permanent after its being in existence for nearly 40 years. Until this point, American politicians and diplomats had hoped to restore formal relations with Cuba. But by making the embargo permanent, the United States signaled that it believed that Castro would never relax his grip on the people and cease his human rights violations. The U.S. determined that Castro was unfit to lead Cuba out of its fiscal problems and decided to waste no further efforts making peace.

Part of this decision was the response of the Cuban-American population regarding the breakdown of immigration talks. Those who had fled Cuba wanted to see Castro punished for his years of abuse, and the United States was unwilling to do so directly. The only real option that the U.S. had was to formalize the embargo, which had little economic or politic effect but appeased the Cuban-American population. The announcement had little effect on the lives of Cubans living in Cuba, as the economy had been largely ruined by the Special Period in the 1980s.

42) 1998 - Pope John Paul II Visits Cuba

The Catholic Church has a long history of sending envoys to countries that are suffering or are in need. An example of this is the Pope's visitation of Poland during the 1970s even though the country was under a communist regime. In this same vein, Pope John Paul II made history in 1998. He became the first Pope ever to visit Cuba, and it marked the first time since Castro's takeover that a Pope had even been invited.

John Paul II, ever the humanitarian, visited the country in hopes of improving Cuba's relationship with the world. Given the Pope's success in Poland and other places, it seemed that a visit to Cuba would have similar effect. While the United States did indeed lend its support to the visit, it refused to revisit the trade embargo. Castro, in an attempt to improve relations with the world, gave the Cuban population a holiday in order that as many people as possible could see the Pope during his visit.

In one sense, the visit was a success as the Pope brought a measure of hope and dignity to the Cuban people, but in another sense the visit was a failure, as no material changes (neither internal nor external) occurred.

43) 1999 - Elian Gonzalez Legal Battle

In 1999, a young woman named Elizabeth Gonzalez along with her boyfriend, her young son Elian, and several others attempted to flee Cuba for the United States. On the journey, Elizabeth died when the boat carrying the group sank. Only her son and two others survived. They were discovered by fishermen and turned over to the U.S. Coast Guard. Thus began a legal battle: Elian Gonzalez was placed with family members in Miami, even though his feet had not been "dry" and in theory could be returned to Cuba. Complicating things further, his family in Miami petitioned to have him remain in the United States while his father back in Cuba petitioned to have him returned.

This case was important for America's immigrant policy, as it would set precedent for the years to come. Eventually, it was ruled that Elian would be returned home to Cuba, and he was deported. The popular opinion regarding this decision was widely split, as many were opposed to returning a person to Cuba. However, there were others who praised the decision, as it was a step toward immigration reform that many had been seeking.

44) 2000 - United States Approves Food and Medical Sales in Cuba

In 2000, the United States Congress passed legislation allowing the sale of food and medicine in Cuba. Although the embargo remained in place, this marked a first in Cuban-American relations since 1962, when the embargo was first enacted. This legislation was designed to allow some measure of respite to Cubans who continued to suffer.

Cuban-American politicians, however, set limits on the bill. The embargo would still remain, meaning that no Cuban goods could be sold in America, and American financial institutions would not be allowed to extend credit to Cubans. Given the poor financial state of most Cubans, this meant that relatively little American medicine or food would reach the Cuban population.

Still, this was a first step in mending relations between the two countries, as it meant that America was slowly relaxing its position on Cuba. Over the next several years, relations between the two nations would improve until ultimately formal relations would be restored in 2015.

45) 2002 - Guantanamo Bay Naval Base Used for Interrogation of Suspected Terrorists

In the wake of the 9/11 attacks in the United States, the U.S. launched its War on Terror. The United States Constitution expressly forbids certain forms of punishment, and sets out the rights of those accused of committing a crime. Further, those who have not been found guilty are presumed innocent, and so cannot be subject to punishment until their innocence has been decided. But the fear of another major terrorist attack led the United States to begin extrajudicial proceedings against those suspected of being terrorists, or those having knowledge of terrorist activities.

Since the Constitution forbade most forms of interrogation, the United States had to look elsewhere to hold its suspects. And so, it chose the Guantanamo Bay Naval Base. This was done because the base was on lease (albeit permanent) from Cuba, meaning that it was not a part of America and that the Constitution did not hold sway. Further, as a military base, Guantanamo Bay is governed by the UCMJ (Uniform Code of Military Justice), which does not have the same protections as the Constitution.

From 2002, the United States has used Guantanamo Bay (Gitmo) as a base for interrogating terrorists or those suspected of terrorism. Many nations around the world have called for the United States to give up these practices, as many of them amount to torture (although the United States would never openly admit this). The United States, however, has refused, much to the consternation of many of its allies and a significant proportion of its own citizens. Although Cuba had no direct role in these interrogations, it is worth noting that once again due to its location, Cuba was at the center of much larger world events—a pattern that has become obvious over the past century.

46) 2002 - Former President Jimmy Carter Visits Cuba

Former President Jimmy Carter of the United States has a long history of humanitarian outreach. From Habitat for Humanity to his work in Africa, Carter has spent the years since his presidency trying to improve the lives of the impoverished throughout the world. In 2002, Carter received an official invitation to visit Cuba from Fidel Castro. No current or past president had visited Cuba since Castro had taken office, and this trip was seen as a way to improve American-Cuban relations.

During the trip, Carter met with Castro to discuss the various issues that stood between formal relations between the two nations. As an unofficial representative of the United States, Carter was able to make suggestions where other diplomats would have made demands. Castro, without making promises, at least allowed the dialogue to take place, and was not openly hostile towards many of the suggestions.

Carter also toured hospitals, many of which (despite the poverty of the nation) were quite advanced. He also toured schools and businesses. Although no formal arrangements were made as a result of the tour, it did open the door for improved communication between the two nations.

47) 2008 - Fidel Castro Resigns

From 1959 through 2008, Fidel Castro ruled Cuba with undisputed authority. But even powerful men age; in 2008 Castro was 83 years old. By that time, he had suffered several major medical problems, including two heart attacks. It has been reported that he has even started to suffer from dementia.

Given his progressively failing health, and an inability to maintain the pace necessary to rule a nation, Castro resigned in 2008 and named his brother Raul his successor. Raul, who had been working at his brother's side since the abortive attempt at coup in 1953, was much more moderate than Fidel. Unlike his brother, Raul slowly began introducing change in Cuban society. Although Cuba has maintained a communist government, it has evolved its position over time to permit individuals to own businesses—a distinct hallmark of capitalism. Furthermore, Raul curbed some of the human rights violations of which his brother had been guilty. This is not to suggest that Raul suddenly or magically changed Cuba, but rather that he has been willing to allow Cuban to slowly modernize.

After Raul's reelection in 2013, he announced that when his term ends in 2018 he will retire and not seek another term as president. These actions are indicative of change finally starting to occur in Cuba.

48) 2012 - First Public Religious Holiday since 1959

Another sign of the changes in Cuba came in 2012. At the request of Pope Benedict XVI, Raul Castro ordered that Good Friday become a permanent national holiday. Historically, communist countries have disallowed religious holidays, as communist leaders do not want to allow the people to have religion, which may cause them to revolt. As the power of a communist government fades, often one of the first signs is the appearance of religion and religious celebrations.

Unlike his brother, Raul Castro allowed Good Friday to become a holiday, as he recognized the value of giving the people hope and the opportunity to celebrate their heritage (which, being largely Spanish, was also Catholic). Although steps like these seem quite small, for a nation that remained static for over 30 years, this was a sign that Cuba was finally moving away from the culture established by Fidel Castro. Further, these steps taken by Raul have increased Cuba's status in the eyes of many countries around the world, including its most powerful neighbor, the United States.

49) 2014 - Deep-Water Port Project Started by Brazil

Hoping to entice new businesses to come to Cuba, a massive infrastructure undertaking has begun in within the country. Financed by Brazil, a new deep-water port is being built near Havana. This port will allow Cuba to become part of the trade route that ultimately leads to the Panama Canal. Until the completion of this port, ships that must either divert to Miami or New Orleans prior to reaching the Panama Canal, and both ports are not necessarily convenient for shipping.

This port, which will cost almost a billion dollars when complete, will be the first step in modernizing Cuban infrastructure, helping it join the world as a major industrialized nation. Once again, the location of Cuba has provided it with great opportunity for advancement.

50) 2015 - Diplomatic Relations with United States Re stored

In the wake of the significant changes occurring within Cuba, including Raul Castro's willingness to embrace change and human rights, the United States has pursued a course of reconciliation with Cuba.

On July 20, 2015, the Cuban Ambassador to the United States traveled to the United States and raised the Cuban flag at the embassy, signifying that he had taken up residence, that hostilities had come to an end between the two nations, and that diplomatic relationships had been reestablished. It also marked the end to the American embargo of Cuba, which had gone on for over 50 years. As Cuba moves forward from this point, hopefully it will be able to shed the pain of its past and become a prosperous, thriving nation as it was during its early history. Only time will tell whether Cuba will be able to make the changes necessary to fully exploit the opportunities of the twenty-first century, but given the strides Cuba has made during the past decade there is yet hope for Cuba to become the nation its citizens require.

Made in the USA
Columbia, SC
11 July 2018